T0160414

STATE OF EXILE

STATE OF ——————————————

EXILE

CRISTINA PERI ROSSI

TRANSLATED FROM THE SPANISH BY

MARILYN BUCK

POCKET POETS SERIES NUMBER 58

CITY LIGHTS BOOKS

SAN FRANCISCO

Introduction and translations
copyright © 2008 by Marilyn Buck

Originally published as *Estado de exilio*
(Ediciones Destino, 2003)

Design and composition by Quemadura

Library of Congress Cataloging-in-Publication Data
Peri Rossi, Cristina, 1941–
[Estados de exilio. English]
State of exile / Cristina Peri Rossi ;
translated from the Spanish by Marilyn Buck.
p. cm. — (Pocket poets series ; no. 58)
ISBN 978-0-87286-463-4
I. Buck, Marilyn. II. Title.
PQ8520.26.E74E78213 2008
861'.64—dc22
2007049996

Visit our website: www.citylights.com

City Lights books are published
at the City Lights Bookstore
261 Columbus Avenue
San Francisco, CA 94133

CONTENTS

Translation: Dialogue of Exile

The contemporary world is a place of exiles and refugees; the displaced run like rivers through myriad countries, flowing toward the seas:

> Exile
> is a blind
> river winding
> from country to country
>
> ["IX"]

To leave is not as easy as it may seem. The exile, no matter the circumstances, faces tremendous loss, absence and alien-

ation. A sense of abandoning one's own country, family and friends generates great doubt, sorrow and remorse or guilt, even though the exile knows realistically that survival is a political, social and human imperative.

The exile loses her life in an instant. That moment in which one steps over a threshold, across a border, to disappear, life as it was vanishes. Like trees, human beings find it difficult to be wrenched up, our roots torn away. The vestiges left behind might become incubators for nostalgia, shadowy forms of what was. We cannot help but exist in a state of suspension until we generate new roots. With time, as the shock and nightmares of flight and dislocation recede, that state of suspension becomes one of alienation. If roots are not planted from the cutting of life carried with us, we may become ghosts or tread the seawaters of dreams:

> Through the streets, they pursue
> old shadows
> photos of the dead
>
> ["The Exiled"]

In one's absence, everything changes. Nothing is as it was, not even one's own identity. Forced departure requires a shift in worldview and self. This rupture in self may initially be disguised by the flight, but inexorably translates one's "self" into some different "self," whether or not one desires it. Peri Rossi expresses the grief:

> —hunted birds—
> we lose what we win
> and what we've won
> was lost in the flight.
>
> ["VIII"]

In her sea crossing from Uruguay to Spain, Cristina Peri Rossi carried her journal in which to draw the anguished, visceral portrait of the translation of self and the difficulty of coming to terms with flight and abandonment. The poems in *State of Exile* are the record of this journey, translated through the details.

In her prologue, Peri Rossi states that "pain-castration–integration–love for the adopted city" was the progression of

her journey into exile. In 1972 she left one country for another, one life for another. So long stowed away, this small volume speaks to this experience: the physical and emotional loss and absence, and the decisions to be made in the strange lands in which one may find herself.

State of Exile

Political exile is a location, among places unknown. Flight into exile is rarely an unforced decision; one may be forced by the authorities to leave one's country or may decide to leave because one faces likely imprisonment, or worse. In the case of the military dictatorship in Cristina Peri Rossi's homeland, Uruguay, in the early 1970s, capture was only the prelude to certain torture and possible death.

Exile may also be collective, as in the case of the Palestinian people, forced from their homeland, or the people of Darfur, murdered and driven from their lands. And there is another form of exile as well—internal exile—in which one is taken

from the location of one's home and life and transported to some other outlying, isolated region of their own country. We think of the gulags of the former Soviet Union, for example, or stories from centuries past, but the fact is that internal exile exists here and now in the United States, a country of exiles, refugees and survivors. Prison is a state of exile.

In prison, men and women wait to return to a home that no longer exists, to the shreds of a once-lived life. Everything has changed while time has passed; friends, family, relationships, all are traces of what once was. Release is a date, but does not always deliver one to a place that was home. Therefore, while some wait and plan to return—not unlike many political exiles —others are forced to imagine reassembling their lives in places foreign to their experience—exiles yet again.

Some prisoners resign themselves and stow their imagination in boxes labeled "Open upon release date" and bury themselves in the oblivion of prison culture, despair, religion or television. Some erect lives inside their sentences; only a few admit that prison is their new society, however much of an abomination it may be—for a year, for ten years, for a lifetime.

These prisoners decide to relinquish pretensions of control over what once was, that which was snatched from their grasp and over which they retain little reach. They come to terms with internal exile and guard their identity. They encounter possibility, imagination, desire—the substance of living—and reject victimization. They begin to stockpile independence and nurture their uniqueness. They may fall in love, and even subvert the programmed world of the keepers, at times managing to live beneath the keeper's radar—not so different from the political exile who looks over her shoulder in a strange land; not unlike the experience that Cristina Peri Rossi poetically narrates in *State of Exile*.

This is where I begin, the translator in exile of a translator of exile. My point of view as a political prisoner in internal exile is not so different from Peri Rossi's after she fled the military dictatorship of Uruguay. She went into external exile, while I, a political militant, did not choose external exile in time and was captured. I became a U.S. political prisoner and was sentenced to internal exile, where I remain after more than twenty years.

Because of my own state of exile, Cristina Peri Rossi's journey has great meaning for me. I translate her work because her voice and point of view provoke me, compel me to engage with her thoughts, her emotions. I want others to hear her, to gain understanding about what happened in the past in order to better understand the present.

While thirty years is a very long time in U.S. literary culture, this poetic work has not lost its currency. The United States is not so very different from Uruguay in the 1970s. After all, it provided endless undercover support for the Uruguayan generals then; today it applauds torture as a necessity to uphold the beacon of deluded democracy.

Given the number of people, historically, who have come to the United States as political exiles, the poetry of exile is crucial to an urgent and critical self-examination of the American state. For those who are not able to imagine exile, or those who never have considered it (even though they may be descendants of either exiles or refugees—or both), perhaps this translation of Peri Rossi's verse can lead to questioning or imagining it for themselves.

Exile as Poetic Translation

Translation involves an act of transformation. —Octavio Paz

Translation is a rite of transformation. Generally, it is thought of only as the movement from one language to another; however, "translation" is a more multidimensional word and concept (from the Latin *translatus*, the past participle of *transferre*— to transfer). Transference or translation is the vehicle that links many realms: place to place, one body to another, the senses to the thought to the utterance.

Cristina Peri Rossi connects exile to translation of self. An intimate connection, it begins with forced departure. One removes one's self from one's cultural and social life, launching into alien seas and territories where another life can only be imagined. The exile journeys from one shore to another, and although she may lack a personal language of forced departure, that language emerges from the experience itself, from the need to define what has happened and to imagine how one will survive and live. The act of leaving is transformative and

seeks translation. Peri Rossi finds that through salvaging herself as a writer, she transposes her existence from "what was" to "what would become." She claims this translation voyage through poetry:

> For luggage
> a suitcase full of paper
> and anguish
> the paper
> to write the anguish
> so I might live with it
>
> ["First Journey"]

This poetic journey begins with the tortured Uruguayan homeland. The stark realization of attachment to home is a wound:

> I have a pain here,
>   on my homeland side.
>
> ["I"]

The pain of those left behind, those captured, tortured and killed, is her own, inscribed word by torturous word on a poetic tide that travels from one side of the sea to the other. In "Letter from Mamá," she questions: "What are we who stay going to do?" Later, in "Letter from Mamá II," she relates:

> They told us that things would change
> with the new general
> but if anything changed
> it was for the worse

The voice of those left behind allows us to feel that sense of abandonment from those who stay as well as those who leave. But it is the voice of those forced to flee that emerges page by page, wave by wave, as the human tide of political exiles reaches "the other side."

Loss and absence are difficult to articulate, and Peri Rossi does so by recording the daily details and traumas, expressing the emotional lacerations and subtler repercussions of uprootedness. The language of the exiled and the tortured is disturb-

ing and horrifying for its deceptive everydayness. Common words betray the mercilessness of capturing or kidnapping human beings from a state of ordinary social and political life to cast them into an infernal condition:

> "They raped Alicia five times
> and then left her to the dogs"
> Well trained,
> military dogs
>
> ["XXIII"]

The brutal uprooting of exile does not lend itself to artifice. In terse lines, she dispels any romantic notion one might have of exile:

> In Uruguay he was a mathematician
> he never wanted to go to Europe.
>
> ["XXII"]

Crossing Over

Peri Rossi's poetry is poetry of this real world; her verses are fragments of emotion and memory. They gather, like a shipwreck's planks, and travel on ocean waves toward shore. They are life preservers. She lands in a world of exile where she is virtually a non-person, but as she gains familiarity with that strange world, she begins to accommodate.

The later poems in *State of Exile* accumulate and integrate the cultural and linguistic references gained through her passage and experience. After her years of exile in France (where she was forced to flee from Franco's Spain in the first years of her exile), she returned to Barcelona, which she ultimately adopted as her new home. In "Round Trip" she examines her own dreams of home and nostalgia:

> Might it be this city
> sad at dusk
> faded at six in the evening
> this city from which we cannot set off

For her, loss would be too difficult to bear a second time. In "Gotan," written before the possibility of return to Uruguay existed, she employs tango lyrics—the music of nostalgia as well as part of her homeland's culture—to underscore the impossibility of return:

> There is no return:
> time flies
> space changes
> everything spins in the infinite circle
> of cruel absurdity

Exile and alienation are the malady; desire and love are redemption. Either the exile is frustrated and lives with rose-colored longing for what is gone, or she finds a reason and a passion to live in her present condition. She casts off the possibility of a return to the past (or to an imagined, but still nostalgic future), and desire awakens to nurture itself through love of another place, another person, new possibility. The desire to live, and not merely wait, translates into new creations, leaping over becalmed seas.

Cristina Peri Rossi takes a giant step: she chooses love and a new land, a new home, and opens the doors of her desire to love and living. She transforms her exile into a different language, a language that offers potential for full-blooded life. This is her revelation, and resolution:

> I'm sure that love will be our revenge
> to be able to love, still
> to be able to love, in spite of everything
>
> ["XXIV"]

Love and desire open time and space, thus prevailing over the estrangement and alienation of exile. Her flight ends; she enters another life-place:

> I don't need to go very far
> to dream
> A train to the suburbs is enough for me
>
> ["Proximities"]

The final poem in *State of Exile*, "Barnanit," is the map for her ongoing transformation:

I think that in loving you
I shall learn a new tongue
that ancient language
where autumn is feminine
la tardor—

Through tenacity and the reclamation of desire—our life force—the poet, and the reader, may survive—super survive—both great horrors and not-so-great traumas to truly live in this world as human beings.

MARILYN BUCK

Dublin, California

September 2007

Si el exilio no fuera una terrible experiencia humana, sería un género literario. O ambas cosas a la vez. La etimología de la palabra es muy expresiva: ex significa, precisamente, quien ya no es, ha dejado de ser. Es decir, quien ha perdido toda o parte de su identidad. El exilio cuestiona, en primer lugar, la identidad, ya que desvincula de los orígenes, de la historia particular de una nación, de un pueblo, desvincula de una geografía, tanto como de una familia, de una calle, de una arboleda o de una relación sentimental. Sólo cuando el exilio es colectivo—desde el más remoto, el de la Diáspora judía hasta el exilio de los españoles fieles a la República—se conserva una parte de la identidad, a pesar del cambio de espacio, y entonces, sus símbolos (desde las banderas hasta los himnos, desde la manera

If exile were not a terrible human experience, it would be a literary genre. Or both things at the same time. The etymology of the word expresses a lot: "ex" signifies precisely "one who no longer is," "one who has stopped being." That is to say: one who has lost all or part of her or his identity. Exile calls into question, first and foremost, identity—inasmuch as one is disconnected from one's origins, from the history of a particular nation, of a people; unmoored from a geography as well as from a family, from a street, from a woody grove or from an emotional relationship. Only when exile is collective—from the very remote, such as that of the Jewish Diaspora, to the exile of Spaniards faithful to the Republic—is part of the identity preserved in spite of the change in place. Then its symbols

de cocinar los alimentos hasta la forma de vestir, desde la seducción hasta los pasos de una danza) se cargan de significación: dejan de ser triviales para convertirse en emblemas, en raíces, en anclas. Si vivir es navegar ("Navegar es necesario, vivir no," lema de la Unión Hanseática) el mar es la tierra del navegante, y todo, fuera del mar, es naufragio.

A fines de 1972 mis libros, en Uruguay, país en el que nací, fueron prohibidos, así como la mención de mi nombre en cualquier medio de comunicación y fui despojada de mi cátedra de Literatura Comparada; también se me prohibió escribir en cualquier órgano de difusión. Silenciada, amenazada y perseguida, opté por exiliarme; tenía la esperanza de que fuera por tiempo breve. Alguien que huye no puede elegir en una guía de turismo el lugar adonde irá a parar; el barco y el destino me trajeron a Barcelona. Poco después, tuve que dejar también esa ciudad y residir un corto tiempo en París, hasta regresar definitivamente a España.

Cuando dejé Montevideo a bordo de un barco de bandera italiana (el *Giulio Cesare*, de la Compañía Trasmediterránea) tenía, fundamentalmente, un temor: no poder volver a escribir.

become charged with significance—from the flags to the hymns, from the cuisine to the style of dress, the mating rituals to the dance steps. They are no longer commonplace, they become roots, anchors, emblems. If to live is to navigate ("To navigate is necessary, to live no"—the slogan of the Hanseatic League), the sea is the land of the sailor, and all beyond the sea is a shipwreck.

By the end of 1972, in Uruguay, the country where I was born, my books were banned, along with any mention of my name in any media whatsoever; I was removed from my professorship in Comparative Literature; I was barred from writing for any publication. Silenced, threatened and hounded, I decided to go into exile; I hoped that I wouldn't be gone very long. No one who flees can choose from a tourist guide where she will end up. A ship and destiny brought me to Barcelona. Shortly after, I had to leave this city also; I resided in Paris for a short time. Later, I returned to Spain to stay.

When I left Montevideo aboard the *Giulio Cesare* (an Italian ship belonging to the TransMediterranean Company), I had one deep-seated fear: that I would not be able to write again;

Que mi identidad de escritora sufriera una fractura tan abisal que me indujera al silencio. Dicho de otro modo: el exilio como castración. (La castración con todas sus metáforas es el fantasma que cualquier pérdida pone en evidencia.) Sin embargo, sin darme cuenta, ocurriría lo contrario: como toda experiencia que concierne a la personalidad entera, y a cada una de sus partes, el exilio me pidió palabras, me pidió escritura, me pidió fijar les emociones. Escribí en una especie de diario que llevaba entonces: "Mientras sufro por el temor a no poder escribir más, en el exilio, escribo. Mientras temo la castración, escribo. Mientras padezco el dolor, el desgarramiento, escribo." Literatura y terapia.

La mayoría de los poemas que componen *Estado de exilio* fueron escritos en los años amargos de las dictaduras latinoamericanas, cuando las calles y los albergues de París, Londres, Barcelona, Madrid, Estocolmo y Ontario estaban repletos de argentinos, uruguayos y chilenos que habían salvado el pellejo "en el anca de un piojo," genial metáfora que le escuché una vez a un maduro marinero uruguayo, convertido, por azares de la emigración, en pizzero de un restaurante de la avenida Infanta

that my identity as a writer would suffer a fracture so fathomless as to render me silent. Put another way: exile is castrating. (Castration with all its metaphors is the ghost that loss brings out into the open.) Yet, without my realizing it, the contrary occurred: as with all experience that concerns the whole personality and each of its parts, exile begged me for words, insisted that I write, obliged me to make sense of my emotions. I wrote in a diary that I carried in those days: "While I suffer from the fear that I can't write anymore, in exile, I write. While I fear castration, I write. While I ache and shatter into pieces, I write." Literature and therapy.

The majority of the poems that compose *State of Exile* were written in the bitter years of the Latin American dictatorships, when the streets and the rooming houses of Paris, London, Barcelona, Madrid, Stockholm and Ontario were overflowing with Argentineans, Uruguayans and Chileans who had saved themselves "by a flea's ass," a brilliant metaphor that I heard once from a wise old Uruguayan sailor who, by accident of emigration, had become a pizza maker in a restaurant on the Avenida Infanta Carlota in Barcelona. This was the first book

Carlota, Barcelona. Fue el primer libro que escribí en el exilio, y sin embargo, no intenté publicarlo. Un extraño pudor me lo impidió. No es fácil llorar en las calles de las ciudades adoptivas, y no quería contribuir al dolor colectivo, al desgarramiento solitario. Intentaba evitar, además, la autocomplacencia narcisista, la conmiseración. Por eso, muy pocos están escritos en primera persona. No me interesaba tanto expresar mis sentimientos, mis emociones, sino el fenómeno en sí; miraba el dolor ajeno para dejar de mirar el propio. Si los hubiera publicado entonces, en 1973, cuando fueron escritos en su mayoría, posiblemente habría sido el primero de los libros de poemas del exilio latinoamericano, pero tampoco me interesaba con cursar en fechas; mi experiencia de escritora había confirmado una sentencia de Franz Kafka, dicha a su amigo Janouch: "El arte es, a veces, un reloj que adelanta." Por adelantarme a los acontecimientos yo me encontraba sola, enferma, exiliada, lejos de mi ciudad natal, de mi familia, de mis libros, de mis amigos y de todo aquello que fue mi mundo durante los treinta primeros años de mi vida.

Una vez que el dolor aflojó un poco, comencé a decir que el

that I wrote in exile; however, I didn't intend to publish it. A strange self-consciousness held me back. It isn't easy to cry in the streets of adopted cities, and I had no wish to contribute to the collective sorrow, to the individual heartbreak. I also tried to avoid narcissistic complacency and self-pity. For that reason very few are written in the first person. I wasn't so much interested in expressing my feelings and emotions as in exploring the phenomenon itself; I looked at the suffering outside myself in order to stop looking at my own. Had I published then, in 1973, when most of these poems were written, it might have been the first of the books of Latin American exile poetry, but I wasn't interested in competing over publication dates. My experience as a writer had confirmed for me something Franz Kafka said to his friend Janouch: "Art is sometimes like a clock that runs fast." As far as the events concerned, I found myself alone, sick, an exile far from my birthplace, from my family, my books, my friends and everything that had been my world for the first thirty years of my life.

Once the pain eased a little, I began to express that exile

exilio nos proporcionaba una segunda oportunidad: la de empezar a vivir en otra parte, cuando ya sabemos las dos cosas más importantes de la vida: leer y escribir. (No se consuela quien no quiere. En el fondo, soy una optimista.)

Publiqué, sin embargo, *Descripción de un naufragio* (en la editorial Lumen) en 1974, alegoría en versos de una derrota, de una ruptura, de una separación, es decir, de un exilio, y alegoría, tambíén, de una supervivencia. Por entonces decía que lo importante no era sobrevivir, sino cómo. Sigo pensando lo mismo: hay formas de sobrevivir que no valen la pena, porque nos dejan sin principios, es decir, sin identidad. Luego, publiqué *Diáspora*, el nombre que le di al exilio latinoamericano y que gozó de fortuna: pasó a designarlo en los medios de comunicación. Pero no era un libro triste, ni desolado: de todas las catástrofes, incluida la del exilio, nos salva la libido. Nada se ha perdido definitivamente, mientras no se ha perdido el impulso libidinal. Vale tanto para el golpe militar en Uruguay, en 1973, como para las Torres Gemelas, en el 2001. Y *Diáspora* (reeditado recientemente por la misma editorial, Lumen) es un libro donde predominan el amor y el humor sobre el dolor.

×××

gives one a second opportunity—to begin to live in another place when we already know the two most important things in life: how to read and to write. (That isn't any consolation to those who don't like to. Fundamentally, I am an optimist.)

However, I did publish *Description of a Shipwreck* in 1974 (published by Lumen). It is an allegory in verse about defeat, estrangement, separation—that is, about exile. But it is also an allegory of survival. At the same time, I thought that what was important was not to survive, but how. I continue believing that. There are modes of survival that are not worthwhile, because we are left without our principles, that is to say, without our identities. Later, I published *Diáspora*, the name that I gave to Latin American exile; the term found resonance and was picked up and used in the media. This was not a sad or despondent book; in all catastrophes, including that of exile, libido can save us. Nothing is wholly lost as long as our libidinal drive remains. That is equally true for the military coup in Uruguay in 1973 and for the Twin Towers in 2001. *Diáspora* (recently reissued by Lumen) is a book in which love and humor predominate over pain. Dictatorships are long (the agony of en-

Largas son las dictaduras (lo terrible de soportarlas es, entre otras cosas, que uno no puede saber nunca cuándo van a terminar) y largos son los exilios. Fui escribiendo, entretanto, otros poemas del libro *Estado de exilio* para completar el periplo: dolor-castración-integración-amor a la ciudad adoptiva. Por eso, el libro termina con dos poemas de aceptación y amor a la nueva vida (*Vita nuova*, llamó Dante, salvando las distancias, al enamoramiento; yo creo que un exiliado sólo se integra plenamente cuando se enamora de alguien que ha nacido allí donde llegó para salvarse. Otra vez, la redención por el amor, tema romántico por excelencia).

Las dictaduras pasaron (parece mentira, pero así fue. Por fin, un día pasó Pinochet, pasó Videla, pasó la Guerra de las Malvinas y pasó la Junta Militar Uruguaya, que sibilinamente, nunca quiso decir su nombre, sabiendo que una dictadura sin rostro, sin identidad, es de carácter metafísico: todopoderosa pero innombrable. Es posible que algunos de los militares uruguayos golpistas hubieran leído a Samuel Beckett. A veces ocurren cosas así), pasó el desexilio: el regreso de miles de expatriados a sus añorados países de origen. "Ja soc aquí," había

during them is, among other things, that one can never know when they will end), and exile is long. Meanwhile, I continued to write other poems for this book, *State of Exile*, in order to complete the journey: pain-castration-integration-love for the adopted city. Therefore, my book finishes with two poems of acceptance and love for a new life. (*Vita nuova*, Dante called it— finding new life on falling in love. I think that an exile is fully integrated only when she falls in love with someone who was born in the place where she has fled to save herself. Again, redemption through love, a romantic theme *par excellence*.)

The dictatorships ended—it seems like a lie, but it did happen. Finally, one day Pinochet passed. Videla passed, the war of the Malvinas' ended. And the Uruguayan military junta left, the junta that like the Sibylline oracle, refused to speak its name, knowing that a dictatorship without a face, without an identity, has a metaphysical character: all-powerful but unnameable. Perhaps some of the Uruguayan military putschists had read Samuel Beckett. Sometimes things like that do happen. And the return from exile passed—thousands of expatriates returned to their longed-for homelands. In an unforgettable

dicho al volver un político exiliado catalán, Josep Tarradellas, en frase inolvidable. Fue repetida por miles de hombres y mujeres, durante el desexilio.

Pero mire, yo no regresé. Me quedé aquí. No quería repetir la experiencia de añoranza, no quería sentir una nostalgia diferente. Soy muy querenciosa con mis nostalgias, prefiero tener siempre las mismas; convivo con ellas, no quiero convivir con otras. Sé perfectamente lo que es extrañar una milonga en San Martín y Yatay, los sábados a la noche, no quiero empezar a saber cómo es extrañar Paseo de Gracia o El Bruma, una de mis cafeterías preferidas de Barcelona.

Después, vinieron las pateras. Otros emigrantes, otros errabundos, otros muertos, otros fracasos, otras desolaciones. Uno se exilia para salvar la vida del terror que es la represión y que es también, el hambre, la falta de esperanza. Entonces, decidí que los poemas de *Estado de exilio* dejaran el cajón o ataúd donde estaban encerrados y fueran por el mundo clamando su ira, su dolor, su piedad, sus sentimientos. Se cumplían los cien años del nacimiento de ese otro exiliado, Rafael Alberti, quien, no por azar, pasó parte de su largo destierro en tierras urugua-

statement, Josep Tarradellas, a Catalán political exile, declared: "*Ja soc aquí*" ("I am here"). It was repeated by thousands of men and women upon their return from exile.

But as you see, I did not return. I remained here. I did not want to repeat the experience of longing. I do not want to feel a different nostalgia; I prefer to hold on to the same one. I have lived with it, I do not want to live with others. I already know perfectly well what it is to miss a *milonga* at San Martín and Yatay, on Saturday nights. I don't want to start learning what it's like to miss the Paseo de Gracia or El Bruma, one of my favorite cafés in Barcelona.

Later, the *pateras* came—the rickety rafts and boats from North Africa. Other emigrants, other wanderers, other deaths, other failures, other anguishes. One goes into exile to save one's life from the terror of repression, but also from hunger and the lack of hope. At that time, I decided that the poems of *State of Exile* would not remain in the box, or coffin, where I had shut them up, they would go out into the world crying out their rage, their pain, their compassion, their sorrows. The centenary of the birth of another writer-in-exile, Rafael Alberti,

yas, en Punta del Este, una especie de paraíso donde él creyó encontrar el que había perdido, el del Puerto de Santa María. Cada exilio es diferente, pero tiene algo en común: la nostalgia. Compartí con Alberti el hecho de ser exiliada, el amor al mar (que él llamó, siempre, la mar), la luz de Cádiz (tan similar a la de Montevideo) y el disgusto por la palabra rape (el pez, no el polvo de esnifar).

Decidí presentar ese libro inédito al Premio Internacional Rafael Alberti, convocado por la Fundación de su nombre, y tuvo la suerte de resultar ganador. Aunque mi poesía y la de Rafael Alberti sólo tienen en común el amor al mar, pienso que le hubiera gustado leer este libro, y así opinó también el jurado.

En poesía, como en ningún otro género, el tiempo es árbitro implacable. Treinta años son nada, o son una eternidad. Apuesto por ambas.

CRISTINA PERI ROSSI

Barcelona, 2003

arrived. He, not coincidentally, had spent part of his long exile in Uruguayan territory, in Punta del Este, which is a kind of paradise where he believed that he had found what he had lost in Puerto de Santa María. Each exile is different, but we all have one thing in common: nostalgia. Besides being in exile like Alberti, I shared his love for the sea (which he always referred to as feminine), the light of Cádiz (so like that of Montevideo) and a distaste for the word *rape* (the fish, not the act).

I decided to submit this unpublished book for the Rafael Alberti International Prize, established by the Rafael Alberti Foundation. I had the fortune to win. Although my poetry and that of Rafael Alberti have only the love of the sea in common, I think he would have liked to read this book, and the jury was of the same opinion.

In poetry, as in no other genre, time is an implacable judge. Thirty years are nothing, or they are an eternity. I'll bet on both.

CRISTINA PERI ROSSI

Barcelona, 2003

STATE OF EXILE

Tengo un dolor aquí,

del lado de la patria.

I have a pain here,

        on my homeland side.

Soñé que me iba lejos de aquí
el mar estaba picado
olas negras y blancas
un lobo muerto en la playa
un madero navegando
luces rojas en altamar

¿Existió alguna vez una ciudad llamada Montevideo?

I dreamed that I was going far from here
on a wind-crested sea
waves black and white
a wolf dead on the beach
a raft floating
lights fiery-red on high seas

Did a city named Montevideo once exist?

Carta de mamá:
"Y si todos se van, hija mía,
¿qué vamos a hacer los que nos quedamos?"

Letter from Mamá:
"My dear daughter, if everyone leaves,
what are we who stay going to do?"

Soñé que me llevaban de aquí
a un lugar peor todavía.

I dreamed that they took me from here
to a place even worse than this.

A LOS PESIMISTAS GRIEGOS

Lo mejor es no nacer,
pero en caso de nacer,
lo mejor es no ser exiliado.

It would be better not to be born,
but in case one is born,
it would be better not to be exiled.

Soñé que volvía
pero una vez allí
tenía miedo
y quería irme
a cualquier otro lado.

I dreamed that I returned
but once I arrived
I was afraid
and wanted to go
anywhere else but there.

VII

Una vez emprendimos   pájaro
el vuelo
por eso   continente
nos son ajenos
todos los viajes
todas las tierras
tránsito

Once we took   bird
flight
therefore   continent
are foreign to us
all journeys
all lands
passing through

Del viajero tenemos
la geografía insensata
el acaso del vuelo
—pájaro acosado—
perdemos lo que ganamos
y lo ganado
se perdió en el vuelo.

As travelers we have
an absurd sense of geography
the sudden unforeseen flight
—hunted birds—
we lose what we win
and what we've won
was lost in the flight.

De país a país
el exilio
es un río
ciego.
Vagan por las calles
no aprendieron todavía el idioma
nuevo
escriben cartas
que no mandan
un año
les parece
mucho tiempo.

Exile
is a blind
river winding
from country to country.
They wander the streets
they haven't learned
the new language yet
they write letters
they don't send
one year
seems like a long time
to them.

X

Exactamente
cansada
harta
agotada
irritada
triste
de todos los lugares de este mundo.

Utterly

exhausted

fed up

worn out

irritated

bored with

        every place in this world.

Una casa
un cuadro
una silla
una lámpara
un ligustro
el sonido del mar
perdidos,

pesan tanto como la ausencia de mamá.

A house
a painting
a chair
a lamp
a blooming privet
the sound of the sea
all lost,

weigh as much as Mamá's absence.

A tantos quilómetros de distancia
nadie puede permanecer fiel.
Ni el árbol que plantamos
ni el libro abandonado,
ni el perro,
que vive en otra casa.

No one can remain faithful
so many miles away.
Not the tree we planted
nor the book left behind,
not even the dog
that now lives in another house.

muy pronto tan lejos bastante mal

                                      siempre

dificultad palabras furiosa largo

extraño extranjero qué más el árbol

sólo miro diferente

todo

        fuera más humano

very soon so far away quite badly
                              always
difficulty words furious interminable
strange a stranger what else the tree
if I just look differently

everything
            could be more human.

Ninguna palabra nunca
ningún discurso
—ni Freud, ni Martí—
sirvió para detener la mano
la máquina
del torturador.
Pero cuando una palabra escrita
en el margen en la página en la pared
sirve para aliviar el dolor de un torturado,
la literatura tiene sentido.

No word
no speech
—not Freud, not Martí—
ever helped to stop the hand
or the machinery
of the torturer.
But when a word written
in the margin on a page on the wall
helps to assuage the pain of the tortured,
literature makes sense.

La sangre no llegará al río
si el río cambia de lugar
y los pájaros azules
—tan azules como tu sombra
de mujer en el espejo—
cantan del otro lado del río
confundiendo a los gendarmes.

The blood won't reach the river
if the river changes course
and blue birds
—as blue as your woman
shadow in the mirror—
sing from the other side of the river
confusing the gendarmes.

Y si llegara
si la sangre llegara al río
los pájaros emprenderían vuelo
un pez rojo
sangre derramada
pájaro azul
olas como ojos desorbitados

But if the blood
if the blood were to reach the river
the birds would take flight
red fish
spilled blood
blue bird
waves like eyes rolling wildly

Si llegara
la sangre
emigrada
del abuelo
pájaro
asaetado
no llegará
el vuelo
pájaro azul
sangre de emigrantes

If grandfather's
emigrant
blood
makes it
bird
struck by an arrow
will not
the flight
blue bird
blood of emigrants.

Tía Ángela pregunta por ti
cada vez que viene de visita
y yo contesto con evasivas
¿o se dice evasiones?
El gato saltó por la ventana
y desapareció
cosas de gatos
cosa de personas
La helada quemó todos los árboles
sólo un limonero sobrevivió
solitario en medio de la tempestad
Nos dijeron que con el nuevo general
las cosas iban a cambiar
pero si algo cambió
fue para peor
El almacenero de la esquina murió
un infarto o una embolia

Aunt Angela asks about you
every time she comes to visit
I answer evasively
Or do you say, with evasions?
The cat jumped out the window
and disappeared
the way cats will
the way people will
The freeze burned all the trees
only one lemon tree survived
alone, in the middle of the storm
They told us that things would change
with the new general
but if anything changed
it was for the worse
The shopkeeper on the corner died
a heart attack or coronary

tu abuela Maruja siempre con las varices
y tu hermana con la úlcera
Me pregunto si por allí estará lloviendo
a veces cuento las horas de diferencia
el asunto de los hemisferios
No te olvides de nosotros
que te queremos tanto.

your grandmother Maruja, still with her varicose veins
and your sister with her ulcer
I wonder if it is raining over there
sometimes I count the difference in hours
the ways of hemispheres
Don't forget about us
who love you so.

LOS EXILIADOS

Persiguen por las calles
sombras antiguas
retratos de muertos
voces balbuceadas
hasta que alguien les dice
que las sombras
los pasos las voces
son un truco del inconsciente
Entonces dudan
miran con incertidumbre
y de pronto
echan a correr
detrás de un rostro
que les recuerda otro antiguo.
No es diferente
el origen de los fantasmas.

Through the streets, they pursue
old shadows
photos of the dead
stammering voices
until someone tells them
that the shadows
the steps the voices
are a trick of the unconscious
Then they hesitate
look about uncertainly
and suddenly
they set out running
after a face
that reminds them of some other old friend.
The origin of ghosts
is no different.

Hablamos lenguas que no son las nuestras
andamos sin pasaporte
ni documento de identidad
escribimos cartas desesperadas
que no enviamos
somos intrusos numerosos desgraciados
sobrevivientes
supervivientes
y a veces eso
nos hace sentir culpables.

We speak languages that are not ours
we walk around without passports
or identity papers
we write hopeless letters
that we don't send
we are numerous forlorn intruders
survivors
super-survivors
and at times that
makes us feel guilty.

Take your hands
me enseñó a decir
en el lenguaje oscuro
de un pájaro inglés.
Yo miraba sus ojos
pero no veía nada.

Take your hands
she taught me to say
in the impenetrable language
of an English bird.
I looked into her eyes
but saw nothing.

Aquel viejo que limpiaba platos
en una cafetería de Saint-Germain
y de noche
cruzaba el Sena
para subir a su habitación
en un octavo piso
sin ascensor sin baño
ni instalaciones sanitarias
era un matemático uruguayo
que nunca había querido viajar a Europa.

That old man
who washes dishes
in a café on Saint-Germain
crosses the Seine each night
climbs to his room
on the eighth floor
no elevator
no bath
not even a toilet.
In Uruguay he was a mathematician
he never wanted to go to Europe.

XXIII

Y vino un periodista de no sé dónde
a preguntarnos qué era para nosotros el exilio.
No sé de dónde era el periodista,
pero igual lo dejé pasar
El cuarto estaba húmedo estaba frío
hacía dos días que no comíamos bocado
sólo agua y pan
las cartas traían malas noticias del Otro Lado
"¿Qué es el exilio para usted?" me dijo
y me invitó con un cigarrillo
No contesto las cartas para no comprometer a mis parientes,
"A Pedro le reventaron los dos ojos
antes de matarlo a golpes, antes,
sólo un poco antes"
"Me gustaría que me dijera qué es el exilio para usted"
"A Alicia la violaron cinco veces

A journalist from I don't know where
came to ask us what exile meant to us.
I don't know where the journalist came from,
but all the same, I let him come in
The room was damp it was cold
we hadn't eaten a meal in two days
only bread and water
letters from the Other Side brought bad news
"What is exile for you?" he said
and offered me a cigarette
I don't answer my letters so I don't endanger my family
"They gouged out Pedro's eyes
before they beat him to death, before,
only a little before"
"I'd like you to tell me what exile is like for you"
"They raped Alicia five times

y luego se la dejaron a los perros"
Bien entrenados,
los perros de los militares
fuertes animales
comen todos los días
fornican todos los días,
con bellas muchachas con bellas mujeres,
la culpa no la tiene el perro,
sabeusté,
perros fuertes,
los perros de los militares,
comen todos los días,
no les falta una mujer para fornicar
"¿Qué es el exilio para usted?"
Seguramente por el artículo le van a dar dinero,
nosotros hace días que no comemos
"La moral es alta, compañero, la moral está intacta"
rotos los dedos, la moral está alta, compañero,
violada la mujer, la moral sigue alta, compañero,

and then left her to the dogs"
Well trained,
military dogs
powerful animals
they eat every day
they fornicate every day,
with beautiful girls with beautiful women,
the dogs aren't guilty
you know,
strong dogs,
military dogs,
they eat every day
they do not lack women to fuck
"What is exile like for you?"
Certainly they'll pay him for the article,
we haven't eaten for days
"Morale is high, compañero, morale is unbroken"
broken fingers, morale is high, compañero
women raped, morale continues high, compañero,

desaparecida la hermana, la moral está alta, compañero,
hace dos días que sólo comemos moral,
de la alta, compañero,
"Dígame qué es el exilio, para usted"

El exilio es comer moral, compañero.

sister disappeared, morale is high, compañero,
for two days we've only eaten morale,
of the highest order, compañero,
"Tell me what exile is like, for you"

Exile is to eat morale, compañero.

XXIV

Nuestra venganza es el amor, Véronique,
te dije aquella noche en Pont des Arts,
el frío no hacía temblar las manos
—el frío, el amor—
desear un café con leche calentito que no costara cinco francos
mientras buscábamos dónde diablos
echarnos a dormir esa noche
sin atraer a los flics
y tú chupabas hasta el tuétano
hasta el capullo
el último cigarrillo de la caja.
Es seguro que nuestra venganza será el amor
poder amar, todavía
poder amar, a pesar de todo
a pesar de según sin dónde cómo cuándo
pero antes, te juro—me dijo Véronique—

Love is our revenge, Véronique
I told you that night on the Pont des Arts
the cold made our hands shake
—the cold, and love—
longing for a hot café con leche that wouldn't cost five francs
we continued looking for where the hell
we might sleep that night
without attracting the *flics*
and you sucked away
on the last cigarette in the pack
down to the butt
I'm sure that love will be our revenge
to be able to love, still
to be able to love, in spite of everything
in spite of circumstances without where when how
but first, I swear to you—Véronique said to me—

me gustaría
me gustaría mucho
mandar a la mierda a unos cuantos hijos de puta,
de manera indolora, claro está,
porque soy civilizada
y hago el amor con preservativo.

I would like
I would really like
to send some of those sons of bitches to hell,
painlessly, of course,
because I am civilized
and I make love with a condom.

CABINA TELEFÓNICA 1975

El exilio es tener un franco en el bolsillo
y que el teléfono se trague la moneda
y no la suelte
—ni moneda, ni llamada—
en el exacto momento en que nos damos cuenta
de que la cabina no funciona.

Exile is having one franc in your pocket
and dropping it into a pay phone
that swallows and doesn't return it
—no money, no call—
at the exact moment you realize
the phone is out of order.

No tuve tiempo de traerme nada,
¿sabe?
Salí muy deprisa,
no tuve tiempo de mirar las cosas
para ver qué me traía,
pero ahora que usted me lo pregunta,
si hubiera podido,
me habría traído al perro.

I didn't have time to bring anything
You know?
I left in a real hurry,
I didn't have time to look things over
to see what I should bring
but now that you ask me,
if I could have,
I would have brought the dog.

El exilio es gastarnos nuestras últimas
cuatro pesetas en un billete de metro para ir
a una entrevista por un empleo que después
no nos darán.

Exile is to spend our last
four *pesetas* for a metro ticket
to go interview for a job
they won't give us.

El hombre estaba tristón,
en medio del bulevar Saint-Germain
sin decidirse
una dirección y otra.
Estas calles son distintas a mis calles,
pensó,
estas palabras son diferentes a mis palabras,
pensó
Dónde he venido a parar,
si mi abuelo lo supiera,
si él me viera,
parado en Saint-Germain-des-Près
sin hablar una jota de francés,
perdido entre los metros
las estaciones los bonos-bus
si mi abuelo lo hubiera sabido

The man stood, dismal,
in the middle of the Boulevard Saint-Germain
unable to decide
which direction to go.
These streets are different from my streets,
he thought,
these words are different from my words,
he thought,
What have I come to?
If my grandfather knew,
if he could see me
standing on Saint Germain-des-Prés
unable to speak one word of French,
lost among the metros
the stations the buses
if my grandfather had known
he would have told all his friends

—soy el primero de la familia que pisó París—
lo habria contado a sus compañeros
y todavía me hago famoso,
pensó,
el cinco de noviembre de mil novecientos setenta y cuatro
parado en el bulevar de Saint-Germain
muerto de hambre y de frío
sin saber una jota de francés.

—I am the first in our family
to set foot in Paris—
and still I'd be famous there, back home,
he thought,
standing on Boulevard Saint-Germain
on November fifth, nineteen hundred seventy-four
dying of hunger and cold
unable to speak a word of French.

XXIX

Compañera no tengo, no, señor.
Nos dijeron que venían hacia la fábrica
pero de allí no se fue nadie, no se fue nadie, le digo,
nadie se movió,
no teníamos armas,
algunos palos y latas,
vinieron con tanques y carros de guerra,
a la primera ráfaga vi volar la cabeza de Santiago,
agarrando todavía la lata que tenía en la mano,
¿cómo quiere que le cuente eso en francés
a una compañera?

No sir, I don't have a girlfriend . . .
They told us that they came toward the factory
but no one left no one left there, I tell you,
no one moved,
we didn't have any weapons,
just some sticks and signs,
they came with tanks and troop trucks,
at the first flash I saw Santiago's head fly off
still holding the sign he had in his hand,
how can I say that in French
to a girlfriend?

×××

Un día yo iba por una calle,
estaba sin empleo y muy nervioso,
iba por una calle en busca de una de esas casas
donde los muertos de hambre dormimos sin pagar
cansado y muy nervioso
y de pronto vi a una pareja
un matrimonio maduro
elegante bien vestido
ropa cara ropa fina
eran turistas comprando cosas y mirando todo
miraban las tiendas de moda y las peluquerías
y los restaurantes
eran turistas
hablaban uruguayo, igual que yo,
yo estaba muy nervioso ese día,
ellos se veía que habían comprado muchas cosas,

XXX

One day I wandered the street,

I was jobless and quite nervous

I wandered the street searching for one of those houses

where the starving might sleep without paying

I was tired and very nervous

suddenly I saw a couple

a middle-aged couple

elegant well-dressed

fine clothes expensive clothes,

they were tourists,

window-shopping buying things

looking at the fashionable shops and hair salons

at restaurants

they were tourists

they spoke like Uruguayans, like I do,

I was very nervous that day,

you could see they'd bought a lot of things,

me reconocieron por la cara
—la cara de la desgracia, según Onetti—
"Usted es uruguayo, ¿verdad?" me dijeron
yo negué con la cabeza, firmemente:
"Soy francés, señores," les dije,
"muy francés, tan francés como la torre Eiffel"
y me fui porque si los mataba
me llevaban preso.

they recognized me by my face
—the face of adversity, as Onetti[1] said—
"You're from Uruguay, aren't you?" they said
I shook my head firmly, no:
"I'm French," I said,
"very French, as French as the Eiffel Tower"
and I left because if I killed them
I would be taken prisoner.

1. Juan Carlos Onetti, a Uruguayan writer whose novels re-created the existential drama of the urban man and woman.

XXXI

Algunos se han dejado crecer la barba,
otros, se han cortado la barba
hay quien se pierde caminando
por no poder dormir,
y hay quienes duermen demasiado,
unos vuelven en rumorosos barcos de humo
que no los llevan al país abandonado
—al país perdido—
y otros vuelven todos los días
con la imaginación.
Se reconocen por el acento,
y por la tristeza de la mirada.

Some have let their beards grow
others have cut off their beards
some lose themselves walking
because they can't sleep,
then there are those who sleep too much,
some return on whispering misty ships
that never take them to the country forsaken
—the country lost—
others return every day
in their imagination.
They recognize each other by their accent,
and by the sadness of their gaze.

Lo llamaban La Momia. Con dos golpes
era capaz de matar a alguien.
Lo usaban para ablandar
a los recién llegados,
o para terminar con los torturados.
No comía pescado
porque una vez se había pinchado
con una espina
y le dolió.

He was called "The Mummy." He could kill
someone with two blows.
They used him to soften up
recent arrivals,
and to finish off the tortured.
He wouldn't eat fish
because once he had been stuck
by a bone
and it hurt.

Bautizan todas las cosas
con los nombres que recuerdan
que vienen del otro lado del mar
pedazos de un lenguaje otro
distinto al que se habla,
y en sus casas,
las plantas, los muebles,
los ceniceros y los gatos
tienen otro nombre.

They baptize everything
with names they remember
that come from the other side of the sea
pieces of another language
different from the one spoken here.
And in their houses,
plants, furniture,
ashtrays, and cats
all have other names.

Extrañan
el ritmo de las ciudades
el cielo opaco lleno de humo
el canto de los pájaros
extrañan el paso de las horas
el calor y el frío
a veces dicen una palabra por otra
y se asustan
cuando descubren que olvidaron
el nombre de una calle.
Se exilian de todas las ciudades
de todos los países
y aman las imágenes de los barcos.

They miss
the rhythm of the cities
the opaque smoke-filled sky
the birds' songs
they miss the passing of the hours
the heat and the cold
sometimes they say one word for another
and are frightened
when they discover that they've forgotten
a street name.
They are exiles from every city
and every country
and they love pictures of ships.

XXXV

Sueñan con volver a un país que ya no existe
y que no reconocerían más que en los mapas
de la memoria
mapas que confeccionan cada noche
en la niebla de los sueños
y que recorren en naves blancas
perpetuamente en movimiento.

Regresan todos los días en el vuelo
de pájaros que se pierden
del cielo de sus ojos
o regresan en caballos alados,
de crines como llamas.

Si volvieran
no reconocerían el lugar
la calle, la casa

They dream about returning to a country that no longer exists
that they would recognize only in the maps
of their memory
maps that they form each night
in the fog of their dreams
maps they travel, in white ships
perpetually in motion.

They return every day on flights
of birds that disappear
in the skies of their eyes
or they return on winged horses,
with blazing manes.

If they returned
they wouldn't know the place,
the street, the house

dudarían an las esquinas
creerían estar en otro lado.

Pero vuelven cada noche
en las naves blancas de los sueños
con rumbo seguro.

they would stand on street corners, in doubt
thinking they were somewhere else.

But each night they return
on their white ships of dreams
sure of the way.

XXXVI

Su regreso sería
el viaje hacia las fuentes
la contraodisea
en naves apocalípticas.
Dirían que es
como si los años no hubieran pasado nunca.

Their return would be
a voyage toward their source
a counter-odyssey
on apocalyptic ships.
They would say it is
as if the years had never passed.

Me gustaría
poder decirte:
Ven cuando quieras,
te estaré esperando.
Los barcos son así
son así los muelles
y los viajeros

Te lo juro
me gustaría
poder decirte
La nave que emprendimos
nos estará esperando
los días pasados
son como si no hubieran pasado nunca
las calles recorridas
están en el mismo lugar
las plazas

I would like to be
able to tell you:
Come when you want,
I'll be waiting for you.
Ships are like that
docks are like that
and travelers.

I swear
I would like to be
able to tell you
The ship we sailed on
will be waiting for us
the days that have passed
will be as if they had never happened
the streets we trod
remain in the same place
the plazas

las fuentes
los árboles
cosas de la imaginación
cosas de la evocación
cosas de la nostalgia
Me gustaría poder decirte
esta mañana llueve
te estaré esperando
como si nada hubiera pasado nunca
como si Pinochet no hubiera asaltado la Casa de la Moneda
como si te hubieras ido hace sólo media hora
a comprar tabaco.

Me gustaría poder decirte
la vida está muy cara
pero los atardeceres siguen siendo rosa
hay niñas que quisieran ser palomas
pero deben ir al colegio
palomas que tienen tu gracia al despertar
tu gracia dormida

the fountains
the trees
objects of the imagination
evocative
nostalgic
I would like to be able to tell you
that this morning it's raining
and I will be waiting for you
as if nothing had ever happened
as if Pinochet had not assaulted the Casa de la Moneda
as if you'd gone out to buy tobacco
only half an hour ago.

I would like to be able to tell you
life is very expensive
but dusk still falls rose-drenched
there are young girls who would like to be doves
but they must go to school
doves that have your grace on waking
your sleeping grace

que es una gracia que no conocen
más que los que te vieron dormida una noche de verano
durante seis años
como yo.
Pero seguramente el hecho
de haberte visto dormida todas las noches de seis años
justamente me impide decirte:
Ven cuando quieras
Te estaré esperando
y seguramente
haberte visto dormida todas las noches de seis años te impide
volver al banco vacío
a la casa abandonada
al barco hundido.
Aunque sepas oscuramente
en las noches de invierno y de verano
que te estaré esperando
como si todas las cosas del mundo
ya nos hubieran pasado para siempre.

a grace known only to those

who saw you sleeping on a summer's night

as I did

for six years.

But undoubtedly the very fact

that I saw you sleeping every night for six years

holds me back from telling you:

Come when you want

I will be waiting for you

and undoubtedly

my having seen you sleeping every night for six years

keeps you from returning

to the vacant bench

the abandoned house

the sunken boat.

Even though, through the winter nights

and summer nights

you might vaguely know

that I will be waiting for you

as if everything in the world

had happened to us already, forever.

EL ARTE DE LA PÉRDIDA
(ELIZABETH BISHOP)

El exilio y sus innumerables pérdidas
me hicieron muy liviana con los objetos
poco posesiva
Ya no me interesa conservar una biblioteca numerosa
(*vanidad de vanidades*)
ni colecciono piedras
botellas cuadros
encendedores
plumas fuentes—así se llamaban en mi infancia
las codiciadas e inasequibles estilográficas
Parker y *Mont Blanc*—
ni necesito un amplio salón para escribir
al abrigo de los ruidos de la calle
y de los ruidos interiores

El exilio y sus innumerables pérdidas
me hicieron dadivosa

Exile and its innumerable losses

made me casual about objects

not so possessive

I am not interested in having a large library now

(vanity of vanities)

nor in collecting rocks

bottles paintings

cigarette lighters

fountain pens—as they were called in my childhood,

those coveted but unattainable

Parker and Mont Blanc pens—

nor do I need a large room in order to write

sheltered from street noises

and indoor sounds

Exile and its innumerable losses

have made me lavish

Regalo lo que no tengo—dinero, poemas, orgasmos—
Quedé flotando—barco perdido en altamar—
con las raíces al aire
como un clavel sin tronco donde enlazarse

El exilio y sus innumerables pérdidas
me hicieron dadivosa
Regalo lo que no tengo—dinero, poemas, orgasmos—
me dejó las raíces al aire
como los nervios de un condenado

Despojada
desposeída
dueña de mi tiempo
Y con él tampoco soy avara:
sería ridículo pretender administrar
un bien desconocido.

I give away what I don't have—money, poems, orgasms—
I'm still floating—a ship lost on high seas—
my roots exposed to the wind
like a carnation without a stalk to cling to

Exile and its innumberable losses
have made me lavish
I give away what I don't have—money, poems, orgasms—
my roots exposed to the wind
like the nerves of a condemned prisoner

Deprived
dispossessed
master of my time
and even with that I am unstinting
it would be ridiculous to try to control
an unknown quantity.

EL VIAJE

Mi primer viaje
fue el del exilio
quince días de mar
sin parar
la mar constante
la mar antigua
la mar continua
la mar, el mal
Quince días de agua
sin luces de neón
sin calles sin aceras
sin ciudades
sólo la luz
de algún barco en fugitiva
Quince días de mar
e incertidumbre
no sabía adónde iba

My first journey
was into exile
fifteen days at sea
without landing
the constant sea
the ancient sea
the sea, sickness
Fifteen days of water
without neon lights
without streets without sidewalks
without cities
only the light
of some other fugitive ship
Fifteen days of sea
and uncertainty
not knowing where I was going
not knowing destiny's port

no conocía el puerto de destino
sólo sabía aquello que dejaba
Por equipaje
una maleta llena de papeles
y de angustia
los papeles
para escribir
la angustia
para vivir con ella
compañera amiga

Nadie te despidió en el puerto de partida
nadie te esperaba en el puerto de llegada
Y las hojas de papel en blanco enmoheciendo
volviéndose amarillas en la maleta
maceradas por el agua de los mares

Desde entonces
tengo el trauma del viajero
si me quedo en la ciudad me angustio

knowing only what I'd left
For luggage
a suitcase full of paper
and anguish
the paper
to write the anguish
so I might live with it
companion friend

No one wished you farewell at the departure
no one waited for you at the arrival
And sheets of paper lay moulding
yellowing in your suitcase
soggy from sea damp

Since then
I have a fear of traveling
if I stay in the city I am distressed

si me voy

tengo miedo de no poder volver

Tiemblo antes de hacer una maleta

—cuánto pesa lo imprescindible—

A veces preferiría no ir a ninguna parte

A veces preferiría marcharme

El espacio me angustia como a los gatos

Partir

es siempre partirse en dos.

if I leave
I'm afraid I can't come back
I tremble at packing a suitcase
—how much does the essential weigh—
Sometimes I would prefer not to go anywhere
Sometimes I'd prefer to just leave
Space makes me as nervous as a cat
To depart
is always to split apart.

LO IMPRESCINDIBLE

Uno aprende que lo imprescindible
no eran los libros
no eran los discos
no eran los gatos
no eran lost paraísos en flor
derramándose en las aceras
ni siquiera la luna grande —blanca—
en las ventanas
no era el mar arribando
su rumia rompedora en el malecón
ni los amigos que ya no se ven
ni las calles de la infancia
ni aquel bar donde hacíamos el amor con la mirada.

Lo imprescindible era otra cosa.

One learns that the essential

wasn't books

wasn't records

wasn't cats

wasn't *paraísos* in bloom

spilling over the sidewalks

nor even the large moon—white—

in the windows

it wasn't the sea lapping the shore

the murmur fragile against the seawall

nor friends no longer seen

nor childhood streets

nor that bar where we made love with our eyes.

The essential was something else.

Para recordar
tuve que partir.
Para que la memoria rebosara
como un cántaro lleno
—el cántaro de una diosa inaccesible—
tuve que partir.
Para pensar en ti
tuve que partir.
El mar se abrió como un telón
como el útero materno
como la placenta hinchada
lentas esferas nocturnas brillaban en el cielo
como signos de una escritura antigua
perdida entre papiros
y la memoria empezó a destilar
la memoria escanció su licor
su droga melancólica

To remember
I had to leave.
So that the memory might overflow
like a full pitcher
—the pitcher of some remote goddess—
I had to leave.
To think about you
I had to leave.
The sea opened like a curtain
like the maternal womb
like the swollen placenta
slow, nocturnal spheres glowing in the sky
like ancient hieroglyphs
lost among papyrus scrolls.
And memory began to distill
to spill its liquor
its melancholic drug

su fuego
sus conchas nacaradas
su espanto
su temblor.
Para recordar
tuve que partir
y soñar con el regreso
—como Ulises—
sin regresar jamás.
Ítaca existe
a condición de no recuperarla.

its fire
its mother-of-pearl
its terrors
its tremors.
To remember
I had to leave
and dream about return
—like Ulysses—
without ever returning.
Ithaca exists
as long as you never go back.

GEOGRAFÍA

Vuelvo con pequeños trofeos en la mano:
un bolígrafo del Banco
un calendario de bolsillo
un encendedor publicitario
un billete de metro sin usar

Los nuevos objetos
triviales, perecederos,
son mi mapa, mi nueva geografía:

a través de ellos
sé qué camino he recorrido hoy
qué calles he visitado
qué espacio he transitado

El billete de metro
el recibo del Banco

I return, small trophies in hand:
a ballpoint pen from the bank
a pocket calendar
a promotional lighter
an unused metro ticket

These new objects,
trivial, perishable
are my map, my new geography:

through them
I know what route I've traveled today
what streets I've visited
what space I've explored.

The metro ticket
the bank receipt

la moneda con una efigie diferente
la ficha para llamar:

guías menos sublimes que Virgilio
para este viaje a Lo Desconocido
a la Nueva Ciudad
a sus paraísos de sex-shop
grandes almacenes
y preservativos de colores.

the different-faced coins
the calling card:

guides, less sublime than Virgil
on this trip to the Unknown
to the New City
with its sex-shop paradises
its giant department stores
and many-colored condoms.

GEOGRAFÍA II

En la ciudad donde nací
de pequeña viajaba en tranvía
grandes cigüeñas de pico de metal

En la nueva ciudad
espero en el andén.
Iluminado y vacío
parece una sala de hospital:
jeringuillas
algodones
esputos

Como en un cuadro nocturno de Hopper
una muchacha solitaria
espera junto a un pilar.

In the city where I was born,
as a child I rode the streetcars
large, metal-beaked storks

In this new city
I wait on the metro platform.
Illuminated and empty
it seems like a hospital waiting room:
syringes
cotton balls
spit

    Like in one of Hopper's nocturnal paintings
a solitary girl
waiting next to a pillar.

Los andenes solitarios están iluminados.
Hay carteles de películas porno,
anuncios de sedantes
y de bonitos dormitorios para parejas recién casadas.
Un joven fornido, de gorra de colores
mea sin contemplaciones contra la pared
y una punkie de pelo rojo y pantalones de cuero
lía un porro en el último escalón.
Por la boca abierta del andén aparece
la mendiga que duerme todas las noches entre cartones
bajo el rótulo electrónico: "Actividades
culturales: museos-ópera-conciertos.
Consulte cartelera."
El último metro se retrasa
pero nadie tiene prisa.
El tipo fornido ha dejado, en efecto, de mear,
pero seguramente volvería a hacerlo

The empty platforms are lit.
There are billboards for porno flicks,
ads for sedatives
and lovely bedroom sets for newlyweds.
A burly young guy in a multicolored cap
pisses on the wall without ceremony
and a punker with red hair and leather pants
rolls a joint on the top step.
Through the yawning mouth of the platform appears
the beggar who sleeps every night in a cardboard box
beneath the electronic marquee:
"Cultural Activities: Museums-Opera-Concerts.
 Consult billboard."
The last train is late
but no one's in a hurry.
The burly guy has finally finished pissing,
though he will surely do it again

la cerveza le oprime la vejiga, el cerebro
y la punkie podría encender otro porro
con la colilla del primero.
En cuanto a mí,
podría pasar el resto de la vida
sólo mirando
envuelta en la nube de la soledad,
de la diferencia.

beer presses on his bladder, and brain
and the punker might light another joint
from the roach of the first.
As for me,
I might spend the rest of my life
just watching
wrapped in a cloud of solitude,
of difference.

Me vendió un cartón de bingo
y me preguntó de dónde era.
"De Uruguay," le dije.
"Habla el español más dulce del mundo,"
me contestó mientras se iba
blandiendo los cartones
como abalorios de la suerte.
A mí, esa noche,
ya no me importó perder o ganar.
Me di cuenta de que estaba enganchada a una lengua
como a una madre,
y que el salón de bingo
era el útero materno.

She sold me a bingo card
and asked me where I was from.
"From Uruguay," I told her.
"You speak the sweetest Spanish in the world,"
she answered as she continued
smoothing the cards
like worry beads.
For me, that night,
it no longer mattered whether I won or lost.
I realized my connection to a language
as to a mother,
and the bingo parlor
was the maternal womb.

VALOR

Te dije:
"Se necesita mucho valor
para tanta muerte inútil."
Pensaste que me refería a América Latina.
No, hablaba
de morir en la cama,
en la gran ciudad,
a los ochenta o a los noventa años.

I said to you:
"One needs a lot of courage
 for so much useless death."
You thought I was referring to Latin America.
No, I was talking
about dying in bed,
in a great city,
at eighty or ninety years old.

Nací en una ciudad triste
de barcos y emigrantes
una ciudad fuera del espacio
suspendida de un malentendido:
un río grande como mar
una llanura desierta como pampa
una pampa gris como cielo.

Nací en una ciudad triste
fuera del mapa
lejana de su continente natural
desplazada del tiempo
como una vieja fotografía
virada al sepia.

Nací en una ciudad triste
de patios con helechos

I was born in a sad city
of ships and emigrants
a city outside of space
suspended in a misunderstanding:
a river wide as sea
a prairie deserted as pampa
a pampa gray as sky.

I was born in a sad city
beyond the map
far from its natural continent
displaced in time
like an old photo
sepia with age.

I was born in a sad city
of fern-filled patios

claraboyas verdes
y el envolvente olor de las glicinas
flores borrachas
flores lilas

Una ciudad
de tangos tristes
viejas prostitutas de dos por cuatro
marineros extraviados
y bares que se llaman City Park.

Y sin embargo
la quise
con un amor desesperado
la ciudad de los imposibles
de los barcos encallados
de las prostitutas que no cobran
de los mendigos que recitan a Baudelaire

La ciudad que aparece en mis sueños
accesible y lejana al mismo tiempo

green-lit skylights
the wisteria's fragrant embrace
drunken flowers
and violet blossoms

A city
of sad tangos
old hookers in two-four time
lost sailors
and bars called City Park.

Nevertheless
I loved her
with a hopeless love
this city of impossibilities
of boats run aground
hookers who don't charge
and beggars who recite Baudelaire

The city that appears in my dreams
within reach and at the same time, remote

la ciudad de los poetas franceses
y los tenderos polacos
los ebanistas gallegos
y los carniceros italianos

Nací en una ciudad triste
suspendida del tiempo
como un sueño inacabado
que se repite siempre.

the city of French poets
and Polish storekeepers
Spanish cabinetmakers
and Italian butchers

I was born in a sad city
suspended in time
like an unfinished dream
that always returns.

Sin saberlo
partimos de la misma ciudad
Sin saberlo
el mismo día
—tú hacia el Norte, yo, hacia el Sur—.

Sin saberlo
sin decirnos nada
regresamos después de tres años
al punto de partida.

"Siempre estás resfriada," dijiste
—soy fiel sólo a mis males—
Yo alabé la belleza permanente de tu voz

¿Sería acaso esta ciudad
triste al atardecer

Without knowing it
we left from the same city
Without knowing it
on the same day
—you toward the North, I toward the South—.

Without knowing it
without saying a word to each other
we returned after three years
to our point of departure.

"You always have a chill," you said
—I am faithful only to my ills—
I praised the lasting beauty of your voice

Might it be this city
sad at dusk

mortecina a las seis de la tarde
la ciudad de la cual no podemos despegar
como despegan los barcos, los aviones?

"Ellos también regresan"
dijiste
y yo pensé que éramos como ellos,
barcos
trenes
sin destino fijo
que se cruzan en el océano
en alguna estación
en el andén lleno de esputos.

faded at six in the evening
this city from which we cannot set off
like ships, like planes?

"They also return"
you said
and I thought that we were like them,
ships
trains
with no fixed destination
passing each other on the ocean
in some station
on a spit-covered platform.

GOTAN

Yo adivino el parpadeo
de las luces que a lo lejos
van marcando mi retorno

No, nadie te esperó, nunca.
No te esperaron los árboles
que habías plantado
ni la estatua del indio herido
en bronce enmohecido
No te esperó tu tía abuela
que murió llamándote
ni la silla de mimbre que vendieron
ni la calle
que cambió de nombre

I can almost see the twinkle of the lights
in the distance
announcing my return[2]

No, no one expected you, ever.
The trees you planted
didn't wait for you
nor the rusted bronze
statue of the wounded Indian
Your great-aunt didn't wait for you
she died calling for you
nor the wicker chair that they sold
nor the street
whose name changed

1. *Gotan* is "tango" in Lunfardo, a working-class dialect born on the docks in
Buenos Aires. It is found in many tango lyrics.
2. Opening verse of *Volver*, a famous tango by Alfredo La Pera and Carlos
Gardel.

El mar no espera nunca
y en su ir y venir
no hay *Arrabal amargo*
no hay *Mi Buenos Aires querido*
cuando yo te vuelva a ver

No está Osvaldo Soriano con su gato
recogido en la rue
que maullaba en francés

ni la dulce francesita que te salvó de los flics
una noche de invierno, en París

No está Raquel que vendía periódicos
y preservativos y sabía el nombre de los árboles
aún de los más viejos.

The sea never waits
and in its coming and going
there is no *Arrabal Amargo*
there is no *My beloved Buenos Aires*
when will I see you again[3]

Osvaldo Soriano[4] is not there with his cat
picked up in a Paris street
that meowed in French

Nor the sweet French girl who saved you from the *flics*
one winter night, in Paris

Nor Raquel who used to sell newspapers
and condoms and knew the names of the trees
even the oldest ones.

3. Titles of popular tangos. *Arrabal* is a barrio of the working class and poor.
4. Contemporary Argentine journalist and novelist, he wrote of the tragic in life with a sense of the absurd.

No adivino el parpadeo de las luces
que a lo lejos van marcando mi retorno

No hay retorno:
el espacio cambia
el tiempo vuela
todo gira en el círculo infinito
del sinsentido atroz

No quiero volver con las sienes marchitas
las nieves del tiempo platearon mi sien

No quiero un arrabal amargo metido en mi vida
como una condena de una maldición
ni que tus horas sombrías torturen mis sueños

No quiero que el camarero del Sorocabana
me pregunte, treinta años después: "¿Un capuchino,
como siempre?"
Siempre no existe,

No, I don't *almost see the twinkle of lights*
in the distance marking my return

There is no return:
time flies
space changes
everything spins in the infinite circle
of cruel absurdity

I don't want *to return with faded temples*
the snow of time silvering my brow

I don't want *Arrabal Amargo dropped into my life*
like a curse
nor do I want *your gloomy hours torturing my dreams*

I don't want the Sorocabana waiter
to ask me thirty years later: "Cappuccino,
like always?"
Always doesn't exist,

Gardel murió,
y la Tana Rinaldi también emigró.
Quiero otra luz, otro mar,
otras voces, otras miradas
romper este pacto de nostalgia
que nos ata, *como una condena de una maldición*
y no volver a soñar con el barco que atraviesa una mar
oscura
para devolverme a la ciudad donde nací.
No hay *Volver*
no hay *arrabal*
Sólo la soledad es igual a sí misma.

Gardel[5] died,
and Tana Rinaldi[6] emigrated.
I want other lights, another sea,
other voices other gazes
to break this pact with nostalgia
that binds us, *like a curse*
I don't want to dream once more of a ship crossing
a dark sea
to take me back to the city where I was born.
There is no *Volver*
there is no *arrabal*
Only loneliness is its same old self.

5. A popular tango singer-composer, Carlos Gardel died at age 40 in a plane crash. He is idolized in Argentina and Uruguay.

6. Susana Rinaldi, a famous tango singer known as "La Tana." *Tano/a* is a term of affection used in Argentina and Uruguay for those of Italian descent.

CERCANÍAS

No necesito ir muy lejos
para soñar
Un tren de cercanías me basta
Unas vías herrumbrosas que corren
al borde del mar
y ya me siento en otro mundo
Mi ignorancia de la nomenclatura
me permite bautizar con otros nombres
Mi ajenidad
—soy la extranjera, la de paso—
es la ciudadanía universal de los sueños.

I don't need to go very far
to dream
A train to the suburbs is enough for me
Some rusted tracks that run
along the seashore
and I feel I'm already in another world
My ignorance of the nomenclature
allows me to baptize with other names
My foreignness
—I am the foreigner, the passing stranger—
is the universal citizenship of dreams.

Creo que por amarte
voy a amar tu geografía
—"una fea ciudad fabril"
la llamó su poeta, Joan Maragall—
la avenida que la atraviesa diagonalmente
como un río inacabable
las fachadas de los edificios llenos de humo
bajo los cuales
—palimpsestos—
se descubren dibujos antiguos
inscripciones romanas

Creo que por amarte
voy a aprender la lengua nueva

I think that in loving you
I shall love your geography
—"an ugly manufacturing city"
your poet Joan Maragall called it—
the avenue that crosses her diagonally
like an endless river
the facades of buildings covered by soot
under which
—palimpsests—
are discovered ancient
Roman inscriptions

I think that in loving you
I shall learn a new tongue

---

1. *Barna* is a Catalonian abbreviation for Barcelona; *nit* is "night": "Barcelona at Night"

esta lengua arcaica
donde otoño es femenino
—*la tardor*—
y el viento helado
tramonta la montaña.

Creo que por amarte
voy a balbucear los nombres
de tus antepasados
y cambiar un océano nervioso
y agitado—el Atlántico—
por un mar tan sereno
que parece muerto.

Creo que por amarte
intercambiaremos sílabas y palabras
como los fetiches de una religión
como las claves de un código secreto
y, feliz, por primera vez en la ciudad extraña
en la ciudad otra,

that ancient language
where autumn is feminine
—*la tardor*—
and the icy wind
crosses over the mountains.

I think that to love you
I will stammer out the names
of your ancestors
and trade the churning
nervous Atlantic ocean
for a sea so serene
it seems dead.

I think that in loving you
we will exchange syllables and words
like religious amulets
like keys to a secret code
and, happy for the first time in this foreign city
this other city,

me dejaré guiar por sus pasajes
por sus entrañas
por sus arcos y volutas
como la viajera por la selva
en el medio del camino de nuestra vida.
Las ciudades sólo se conocen por amor
y las lenguas son todas amadas.

I will let myself be guided through her passages
through her entrails
through her arches and whorls
like a traveler in the forest
in the middle of our lives' road.
Cities are only known through love
and all tongues beloved.

Considered a leading light of the "Latin-American Boom" generation, CRISTINA PERI ROSSI was born in Montevideo, Uruguay. She was forced to leave her country at the age of thirty-one when her work was banned and her life was threatened by a repressive military dictatorship, and in 1972 she moved to Spain, where she still resides. Novelist, poet and short story writer, Peri Rossi is the author of more than 37 works.

MARILYN BUCK's life has long been directed toward battling oppression. She began her anti-racist activism as a teen in Texas, organized against the war in Vietnam and later aligned herself with the Black Liberation Movement. In 1973 she was convicted of purchasing two boxes of handgun ammunition and was given a ten-year sentence. After serving four years in federal prison, she was granted a furlough and did not return. In 1985 Buck was recaptured and convicted of conspiracy in the successful escape of Assata Shakur from her New Jersey prison. She is currently serving a sentence of eighty years at the federal prison in Dublin, California, where she is deeply involved in cultural and educational activities for prisoners, and translates for Spanish-speaking women inside. In 2001 she won the PEN Prison Writing Program poetry prize and published a collection of poems titled *Rescue the Word*.